MISSION FRIENDSHIP

Written by
Serena Patel

Illustrated by
Miriam Serafin

ISBN: 9781036001209

Text © Serena Patel
Design, illustrations and layout © 2025 Hodder & Stoughton Limited
First published in 2025 by Hachette Learning,
An Hachette UK Company
Carmelite House, 50 Victoria Embankment, London EC4Y 0DZ

www.HachetteLearning.com
The authorised representative in the EEA is Hachette Ireland, 8 Castlecourt Centre, Dublin 15, D15 XTP3, Ireland (email: info@hbgi.ie)

Impression number 10 9 8 7 6 5 4 3 2 1
Year 2029 2028 2027 2026 2025

Author: Serena Patel
Illustrator: Miriam Serafin / Advocate Art
Series Editor: Catherine Coe
Educational Consultant: Pauline Allen
Page layout: Rocket Design (East Anglia) Ltd

With thanks to the schools that took part in the development of *Reading Planet Cosmos*, including: Ancaster CE Primary School, Ancaster; Downsway Primary School, Reading; Ferry Lane Primary School, London; Foxborough Primary School, Slough; Griffin Park Primary School, Blackburn; St Barnabas CE First & Middle School, Pershore; Tranmoor Primary School, Doncaster; and Wilton CE Primary School, Wilton.

All rights reserved. Apart from any use permitted under UK copyright law, no part of this publication may be reproduced or transmitted in any form or by any means, electronic or mechanical, including photocopying and recording, or held within any information storage and retrieval system, without permission in writing from the publisher or under licence from the Copyright Licensing Agency Limited. Further details of such licences (for reprographic reproduction) may be obtained from the Copyright Licensing Agency Limited, www.cla.co.uk

A catalogue record for this title is available from the British Library.

Printed in the UK

Hachette UK's policy is to use papers that are natural, renewable and recyclable products and made from wood grown in sustainable forests and other controlled sources. The logging and manufacturing processes are expected to conform to the environmental regulations of the country of origin.

To order please visit www.HachetteLearning.com or contact Customer Service at education@hachette.co.uk / +44 (0)1235 827827

CONTENTS

Chapter One 4

Chapter Two 12

Chapter Three 20

Chapter Four 29

Chapter Five 38

Chapter Six 49

CHAPTER ONE

It all started when Miss Malone split the class up into groups for Geography. Usually, Sita and Sufi would have picked each other to work with, but Miss Malone said that for this project she wanted everyone to work with someone new. Sita was teamed up with the most annoying boy in their class, Valentino. He was the kid that had done everything, been everywhere and knew everything.

"I already have a great idea," Valentino declared as they sat down.

"We don't even know what the project is yet!" Sita replied.

"Doesn't matter – my idea can adapt to any project brief," Valentino answered smugly. "Actually, I have several ideas that I keep in my ideas book for exactly this sort of thing. Do you want to see? I don't show my ideas book to people generally, but you seem trustworthy. Actually, are you trustworthy?" Valentino asked, staring earnestly at Sita.

"This is going to be a nightmare," Sita muttered to herself.

She glanced over at Sufi and rolled her eyes. Sufi smiled back sympathetically as she waited to find out from Miss Malone which annoying person she'd be working with. At least she could laugh with Sita about it on the way home from school.

Sufi and Sita had been best friends since Reception class and now they were in Class 6. They had always done everything together; they were going to the same secondary school in September, too. Sita couldn't imagine ever not being friends with Sufi. Even on the worst day at school, they had each other and that was all that mattered.

Miss Malone continued pairing the children up.

Jax was paired up with Millie, Emilia was teamed up with Zara and then suddenly it was Sufi's turn. "Ah yes, Sufi," Miss Malone said. "You can work with Kiri."

Sita's stomach dipped. Sufi didn't look bothered, but Sita knew this was not good. Kiri smiled sweetly at Sufi and sat down next to her. And then the weirdest thing happened. Sufi smiled back at Kiri!

"Why are you staring at Sufi and Kiri like that?" Valentino asked.

"What? I'm not!" Sita replied, annoyed, while thinking, *Why is Sufi smiling? Kiri is a horrible girl. Sufi knows this!*

Miss Malone walked back to the front of the class. She was talking about the new project.

"We're going to create a map of our community. Not just an ordinary map, but a special interactive one. We're going to interview some of the people who live here – your parents, grandparents and neighbours. We'll look at the history of some of the buildings and really explore the place we all live in. Isn't that exciting?"

Sita wondered if Miss really wanted them to answer that question, because she didn't feel excited about it at all. If she had to say something out loud right now it'd probably be, "No, Miss, it's not exciting. It's actually kind of boring and super annoying because I'm not working with my best friend, and you've teamed her up with the meanest girl in the class. But yeah, sure, let's pretend we're excited. Yay!"

Miss Malone continued, "This piece of work is going to require great teamwork, including some work at home, so make sure you can meet up outside school."

Sita's stomach somersaulted. This was getting worse by the minute. She looked around. Everyone else seemed okay with their teams. Apart from Yaqub and Ali who were giving each other death stares. Everyone knew they were arch enemies and the clueless Miss Malone had teamed them up! Did she know that she'd probably just started the school apocalypse?

Sita raised her hand.

"Yes, Sita?" Miss Malone asked.

"Umm, Miss, can I be put with someone else?"

"Well, the teams are all set now, Sita. Is there any particular reason you don't feel you can work with Valentino?" Miss asked.

Sita's cheeks burned as Valentino stared at her. "Yeah, Sita, what's wrong with working with me?"

"I, um, I don't think there's anything wrong with you but I don't want ... I mean ... I'm worried I won't be able to keep up with Valentino. He's so quick and smart and he has an idea already. He'd probably work better with someone else. I don't want to hold him back," Sita blurted out.

"She's not wrong," Valentino sniffed. "I am all of those things."

Miss Malone smiled kindly at them both. "The point of this project is to work with people you wouldn't normally team up with. It doesn't matter who is quicker with ideas; you're working together, so you both have to compromise and find the best solution."

Valentino groaned. "Compromise? That sounds tedious."

Miss Malone frowned. "Valentino, we've had this chat. Several times."

Valentino groaned again. "Yes, Miss."

Sita slumped in her chair. It was hopeless – she was stuck with Valentino and he was stuck with her. She glanced over at Sufi again, but Sufi wasn't in her chair, and neither was Kiri! Sita scanned the room ...

There they were, over by the bookshelf, picking out books to help with the project. Sufi was laughing at something Kiri said. Sita felt an odd hollow feeling in her stomach. She didn't like it. She didn't like it at all.

At break time, Sita made a beeline for Sufi. She knew she needed to act casual, as if the last hour hadn't been complete torture, watching Sufi having the best time with Kiri while Valentino droned on and on (and on!) about the pros and cons of doing a poster versus presentation slides.

Sufi smiled as she saw Sita approaching and Sita felt herself relax. It was fine; they were fine. The lesson was over and so was Kiri.

Sufi beamed. "Hey, bestie, that lesson was fun, right? I never knew Kiri was cool like that."

Okay, so maybe Kiri wasn't as over as Sita would have liked.

Sita tried to smile but she knew it looked weird. "Oh, yeah, it was okay. I mean I'm paired with Valentino, so, you know, it's educational!" she tried to joke.

"Are you okay?" Sufi asked, touching Sita's arm.

"I ... well ... you looked pretty happy with Kiri." Sita shrugged.

"Are you jealous, bestie?" Sufi grinned. "You know there's only one Sufita!"

Sita smiled. Sufita was what they called themselves – a mash-up of their names. Their mums said they were basically the same person since they finished each other's sentences and loved all the same things. And they both hated tuna: the smell, the texture, the taste! Yuck!

"I'm not jealous. I just wish we'd been paired together. Plus, Kiri *is* horrible. Remember when she made fun of my hair last year after I had it cut? And the time she tripped me up in the playground and then said it was an accident. You were there, you know it wasn't."

Sufi shrugged. "I don't think she's like that any more.

People can change. Anyway, it's one project and it's only until next week. You and me, that's for life."

Sita smiled. "I guess!"

"Anyway, we have so many other important things to chat about," Sufi continued. "Like, Christie has a crush on Jeremiah!"

"Woah, no!" Sita gasped.

"Yeah, Angel told me. And remember when the girls' toilets got flooded because someone shoved a load of paper towels in the sink? I know who did it!"

"Who?"

Sufi looked around and then whispered, "Nazneen!"

"No! She's so quiet!"

"It's always the quiet ones. That's what my mum says," Sufi replied wisely.

Sita laughed. "Your mum says a lot of things."

Sufi laughed too. "She really does!"

Heading back into class, Sita felt much better. Sufi was her best friend. Nothing could ever ruin that, could it?

CHAPTER TWO

The next day, Miss Malone said they'd be working in their teams for the afternoon. She wanted them to plan the project out. She displayed a big map of the local area split into a grid on the whiteboard. Each team was responsible for a square of the grid.

Sita and Valentino got a square that wasn't far from where Sita lived, meaning at least she'd know some of the people who lived there. She noticed they had the library and community centre in their square too.

Valentino, of course, had a million ideas straight away.

"My nan volunteers at the library, so we can talk to her," he said. "She has the best stories. I bet she knows loads about the area."

But Sita wasn't listening; she was watching her best friend. When it was Sufi and Kiri's turn to be assigned a square, they got the easiest one – the one with the school in it!

That meant they didn't even have to walk all round the neighbourhood; they could just run around school.

And there was already a whole display in the corridor about the school, so their work was basically done for them. Sita saw Sufi and Kiri smiling and high-fiving each other, and a knot formed in her stomach.

Valentino nudged her. "You know, the best way to forget about them is to do a really great job on our project. Miss Malone said she'd give a prize for the best team. How awesome would that be?"

Sita sighed, "I guess."

Valentino shrugged. "Whatever ... help or don't help. I'll be at the library and community centre after school on Friday if you want to meet my nan, and we can take pictures and interview some of the people there."

Sita looked over at Sufi, but Sufi was busy laughing and writing stuff down with Kiri. Kiri noticed Sita looking at them though and smirked, covered her mouth and then whispered something to Sufi.

Worst still, Sufi looked in Sita's direction and then burst into a fit of giggles!

Sita's cheeks burned and she blinked back hot angry tears. She turned to Valentino and said, "Okay, V, let's do it."

Valentino grinned. "V. I like it! Team SV – we've got this!"

Sita and Valentino spent the rest of the afternoon writing a list of people they could talk to and finding out interesting things on the laptop about their area. Sita was surprised at how little she knew about the place where she had grown up. Valentino knew loads, of course, but Sita realised that once you got to know him, he wasn't really that annoying.

Sita couldn't help looking over at Sufi and Kiri occasionally though, and every time she did, she regretted it. They were having *the best* time. Sita told herself it was okay; this was just a glitch in their friendship. Deep down Sufi knew Kiri was a bully. Sita didn't like bullies, even ones that were pretending to be nice. Kiri couldn't really come between them ... not properly. Sita and Sufi always walked home together, so they could talk then, and it would all be fine. It was always fine.

Home time seemed to take forever to arrive. When the bell rang, Sita grabbed her stuff from the cloakroom and waited out in the playground for Sufi as usual. Sufi was always the last one out of the classroom.

Today she took an extra-long time, and even Miss Malone was tapping her desk impatiently. "Girls, out you come please. I would like to get home sometime tonight!" she shouted into the cloakroom.

Girls. Plural. As in more than one girl. Sita's stomach lurched. She hadn't seen Kiri leave yet either. And then they appeared, Sufi and Kiri, together. Backpacks slung over their shoulders, walking close together and laughing. Sufi noticed Sita and smiled. "Hey, you didn't have to wait for me."

Sita smiled tightly. "That's okay," she said. But in her head she was thinking, *What are you actually talking about? We always walk home together!*

The three of them walked awkwardly across the playground to the gate. Sita noticed that Kiri made no effort to speak to her, as if she didn't even exist.

As they reached the gate, Kiri turned to Sufi. "So, I'll call you later?"

"Yeah, cool," Sufi said.

As Kiri walked off, Sita tried to act unbothered but couldn't help asking, "So, you're calling each other later?"

Sufi sighed. "Yeah, it's no big deal. We're talking about ideas for our project. Don't make it a thing, okay?"

Sita wanted to cry; Sufi was never like this with her. "I was only asking. If I wanted to make a thing, it would be about how you and Kiri were whispering and laughing at me earlier in class."

Sufi stared at Sita like she didn't recognise her. "What? We weren't! Oh wow, did you think we were laughing at you?"

Sita's face felt very hot suddenly; she hated this. "So, you weren't laughing at me?" she asked in a quiet voice.

"No," Sufi replied. They walked on a bit further in silence.

Sita couldn't leave it though. "So, what were you laughing at?"

Sufi exploded, "Sita, stop! Why can't you JUST LEAVE IT! It was only about the latest Amy Lu video – you know, that vlogger I like. It was nothing about you ... it was literally nothing!"

Sita recoiled. Sufi seemed to see how scared she was and calmed down right away. "Look, I'm sorry, but it's just a project, Sita. Kiri is alright once you get to know her. I told you earlier, me and you, we're best friends. Okay?"

Sita stared at her feet as they landed on the ground, one in front of the other. "Yeah," was all she could get out.

They said goodbye at the corner of Sufi's street. Usually, they'd make a plan to chat later, but Sita didn't even mention it. She knew Sufi had plans to call Kiri. Everything felt wrong. And she didn't know how to put it right again.

As Sita went into her house, the smell of warm rotli and shaak wafted up her nose. Dad came out of the kitchen. "Hey, Beta, how was your day?"

Dad always called her Beta, which was another word for 'child', but meant in the most loving way. Usually it made her feel better, but not today.

"Terrible," Sita replied, and dropped her bag in the hallway. She ran to her dad's open arms and the tears just came.

"Beta, what on Earth could have happened to be this bad?" Dad asked.

"It's Sufi – she's working with this awful girl on our class project, and I got upset, and then Sufi got angry with me, and now I don't think we're friends any more," Sita blurted out in between big heaving sobs.

"Oh no, I'm sorry to hear that, Beta. But you and Sufi have been friends forever. I'm sure that by tomorrow it will all be forgotten."

"I don't think it will, Dad. It was really bad," Sita said sadly, wiping her tears.

"Well, let's see, huh? We won't know until tomorrow. In the meantime, I made your favourite: batata shaak. I did the potatoes a bit crispy, just how you like them. And I made rotli. Of course, they are all different shapes on purpose, not because I can't roll a circular one!" he smiled.

Sita couldn't help but smile back. Dad always knew how to make her feel better. But in the back of her mind, she knew this was no ordinary fallout with Sufi. They never fell out really. And Sufi never raised her voice. The knot in Sita's stomach was getting bigger and bigger.

CHAPTER THREE

The next day was Thursday and that meant PE. Sita hated PE. She just wasn't made for it. She struggled with coordination and mostly ended up hurting herself.

Mr Finch, the PE teacher, split the class into two teams. Sufi and Kiri were on one team and Sita was on the other.

"We're going to play dodgeball. You know the rules. And I'm going to say this once: you should be aiming *below* the shoulders. No head shots, understand?"

"Yes, Sir," everyone replied.

"Okay, get into positions and wait for the whistle."

Sita hated dodgeball most of all. It didn't matter what Mr Finch said, someone always got hit in the face. Usually her.

Sita looked over at Sufi. They hadn't spoken since yesterday. Normally, they walked to school together, but Sufi's mum had phoned Sita's dad this morning and said Sufi had a dentist appointment and would be late.

Sufi glanced over at Sita, smiled and gave her a little half wave. *Maybe we are okay*, thought Sita, breathing a sigh of relief. She waved back. Things would be alright. So what if Sufi enjoyed working with Kiri? It was no big deal. Sita and Sufi had been friends for too long to let someone like Kiri come between them.

Sita stared off into the distance and remembered all the fun stuff she and Sufi had done together: cinema, ice skating, trips to the park with their families. She was so distracted by her memories that she didn't hear the whistle go, nor did she notice the ball approaching her head.

Oof!

"What did I say about head shots?" Mr Finch roared, as he ran over to Sita.

"Sorry, Sir. I have terrible aim," replied a voice.

Sita was in a heap on the floor, but looked up to see that it was Kiri who had thrown the ball. She really didn't look sorry at all.

Sita sat on the bench for the rest of the game and held a cold compress to her head. Sufi didn't come to check on her once. It looked like they were all having too much fun. Kiri was her team's star player, of course, and Mr Finch didn't seem to notice how much of a bully she was, pushing and shoving some of her own teammates even. Worse still, Sufi didn't seem to notice or care either.

As the game was ending, Dina Kaur came and sat next to Sita. "How's your head?" she asked.

Sita grimaced and replied, "Bit sore, but I'll be okay, thanks."

"Kiri's a bully. I don't know why everyone thinks she's so great," Dina said.

Sita looked at Dina. "You think so too? I thought it was just me."

"No, she's definitely a bully. How come Sufi's hanging out with her so much? I thought you two were like sisters?"

"Yeah, me too. They're working on the class project together and Sufi likes being around Kiri. It's only for a short time though," Sita said, trying to convince herself.

"Yeah, that's true," Dina agreed. "Well, I'm stuck without a partner now. I was teamed up with Adnan but he's leaving the school on Friday because his family is moving house. So now I'm by myself!"

Sita had a thought. "You could join me and V. It would be doing me a favour. Valentino's okay but he has *a lot* of ideas!"

"Really? Do you think Miss Malone would let me?" Dina asked.

"Yeah, I'm sure she would be okay with it. You can't do the project on your own. We can ask her next lesson," Sita replied.

She hadn't spoken much to Dina before today; in fact, Sita realised she hadn't spoken much to anyone except Sufi for a long time. Sufi always said they didn't need anyone else. Funny how that had changed in just the last few days.

So, when they returned to class, Sita spoke to Valentino and then to Miss Malone and it was soon agreed: they could work in a team of three. Sita noticed Sufi looking over at them curiously, wanting to know what was going on. That felt good. Maybe she did still care. Sita and Sufi always sat together at lunchtime, so maybe they could put all of this behind them then.

But when lunchtime came and Sita joined the queue, she couldn't see Sufi anywhere. Maybe she was sitting down already. Sita grabbed her tray with a jacket potato, beans and cheese and walked to the tables. No Sufi. Then she heard Kiri talking loudly over by the wall.

She looked to see Sufi sitting with Kiri at the table for people who brought in sandwiches from home. Since when did Sufi bring sandwiches?

She walked over to them. "Hey, Sufi, you don't normally have sandwiches. And is that *tuna*?"

"School dinners are for losers," Kiri answered, even though Sita hadn't asked her anything.

Sufi grinned nervously. "I just thought I'd try it. Kiri likes tuna, so I thought maybe it's not so bad. And you know what? It really isn't. A change is good sometimes, you know. No big deal."

Sita wanted to say, "But it *is* a big deal – you keep saying it's not a big deal, but it feels like the *biggest deal*. Suddenly you like tuna?! Why are you being like this?" But she didn't let out a word. Instead, she said, "Oh, okay, well, umm, I'll see you later then," and she walked away.

It would have been fine left like that if she hadn't tried to do the 'I'm really not that bothered' hair flick that she'd seen the popular girls do a hundred times. Unfortunately, Sita flicked her hair too hard, whacked herself in the face and almost fell into the table she was passing. Not cool at all.

She froze in an awkward pose with one leg in the air and one arm out on front of her. Thinking quickly, Sita tried to make it look like a dance move. As she tried to style it out, Sita heard Kiri snorting with laughter and saying loudly, "Why were you ever friends with her, Sufi?"

Sita could just make out Sufi reply, "Oh, well, our parents are friends – they come to our house a lot."

"I feel sorry for you!" Kiri laughed.

Sita blinked back tears and tried to shake off the horrible hollow feeling in her chest. She wanted to run out of there but instead she looked around for somewhere to sit. Just as she was thinking she'd have to eat alone, Dina and V appeared at her side.

"You okay? Wanna sit together?" Dina asked, smiling.

"Yes please," Sita replied gratefully.

"I saw you over at Sufi and Kiri's table. Forget them," V declared as they sat down. "Sufi's meant to be your best friend, right? How can she ditch you like that?"

"I think she's just confused," Sita said. "She'll come back around."

Dina frowned. "You keep making excuses for her, like she doesn't know what she's doing. But would you want her to come back, after how she's treated you? I heard what she said, making out like you're only friends because of your parents. That's horrible ... and a lie. Are you sure you're still best friends?"

"Of course we're best friends," Sita said. "She's just having a break, I guess. Maybe she didn't mean to lie." Even as she said it, Sita knew that it didn't make sense.

"Well, I wouldn't have it," V said. "You can't just pick friends up and put them down again when you feel like it. That's what my gran says anyway."

Sita knew Dina and Valentino were probably right, but she couldn't just give up on Sufi. This was all just a big misunderstanding. She didn't know what was going on with Sufi or why she was being like this. It was like she'd forgotten that they'd been best friends forever.

That's it! thought Sita. She just needed to remind Sufi of their friendship and how important it was, and then things could go back to normal and Kiri would go away. She didn't say this out loud to Dina or Valentino though. This had to be a covert mission. Only Sita would know the objective. This was Mission Friendship.

MISSION FRIENDSHIP!

CHAPTER FOUR

When Sita got home that evening after not walking home with Sufi yet again, Mission Friendship seemed more important than ever. Sita pulled out her notebook. She needed to make a list. Writing things down always helped Sita when her brain felt too cluttered.

She found a fresh page and wrote:

MISSION FRIENDSHIP

Objective: Get my best friend Sufi back from the evil Kiri.

Plan of how to do this:

Sita sat back on her bed. How could she do this?

Sita thought about their favourite song that she and Sufi always sang for karaoke: 'We Don't Speak Any More!' by the singer Liana. But she had no way of sending it to Sufi, and thinking about it, perhaps it wasn't the best choice of song to send right now. Next, she thought about their favourite pasta that they always had whenever Sita went to Sufi's house. But Sita didn't know how to make it.

Then an idea hit her. She leaned over the side of the bed and grabbed her most prized possession from under it – her photo album. It had hundreds of photos of Sufi and Sita. All the places they'd been and all the things they'd done together. She just needed to pick the right photo to remind Sufi of their friendship. Now which one should it be?

Sita flicked through the pages … hmm, there were so many good ones. The time they went to the fair, the time they had the paddling pool out in Sita's garden, the time they tried to learn how to do cartwheels, the fancy-dress party they went to dressed as a donkey and a monster. It was all there.

Just then, Dad knocked on Sita's door. "Hey, Beta, dinner's almost ready. Oh, your photo album – I haven't seen that for a while!"

"I'm trying to find the perfect photo to remind Sufi of us," Sita explained.

"Remind her of what?" Dad asked, as he sat on the edge of the bed.

"Of us – our friendship," Sita said, still flicking through the album.

"Oh, okay," Dad nodded. "Does she need reminding?"

"Maybe, and I have to do something, Dad. Kiri is taking her away from me. Sufi said I'm overreacting, but I know I'm not. We're never like this: arguing and then not talking. We always have lunch together and she sat with Kiri eating *TUNA*! And she laughs when Kiri makes a joke about me. It's like she's changed overnight into someone I don't know. Maybe she wants me to be more like Kiri, but I don't know how."

"Beta, I'm so sorry Sufi's behaving like that. You have to do what you think is right, but don't forget who you are, okay? You are a great friend – the best friend anyone could want or ask for. A true friend will realise that all by themselves."

Dad went downstairs and Sita sat there for a second thinking about what he'd said. She knew he was right, but she had to try one last time with Sufi.

If it was the other way around, she knew that Sufi wouldn't just give up on her. No way.

The next day, Sita went into school feeling determined. She had picked the perfect photograph, and it was going to get her best friend back. But how would she show Sufi the photo? As Sita filed into class with all the other children, she saw her opportunity. Everyone had a drawer for their pencil case and other bits. Sita's drawer was right next to Sufi's drawer, so she could just slip the photo into Sufi's drawer and then Sufi would see it!

Sita looked around. Everyone was busy getting their own stuff out and finding their seats. She walked over to the drawers, grabbed her pencil case and a notebook from her drawer and then pulled the photo out of her pocket.

But just as she was about to place it in Sufi's drawer, Ella Khan bumped into her and made her drop everything!

"Oh, sorry, Sita!" Ella said, but she didn't stop to help.

Sita crouched down to pick up her things. Where was the photo? She looked around on the floor and saw it had landed under a desk right by ... oh no ... right by Kiri's feet!

Sita tried to reach for the photo, but Miss Malone spotted her.

"Sita, what are you doing down there? Back to your seat please!"

"Yes, Miss. I just dropped something," Sita called out as she ducked her head under the desk and tried to grab the photo. But Kiri noticed her and ducked her head under too.

"Whatchya doing?" Kiri grinned, spotting the photo and grabbing it!

"No ... that's mine!" Sita tried to say, as she banged her head coming out from under the table.

Kiri looked at the photo and burst out laughing. Is that *you* dressed as a donkey? And who's that next to you, dressed as a monster? Is that ... is it Sufi? Haha."

Sufi's face went bright red. "Sita, why is that picture here?" she asked through gritted teeth.

"I ... I was just trying to ..." Sita couldn't find the words. Before she could get the photo back, Kiri had passed it on and then the photo started going round the whole class. Sita wanted to curl up and hide under the desk. "It was a Halloween party. We wanted to go as our favourite movie characters," she tried to explain. But no one was listening, and Kiri was making donkey noises.

Miss Malone clapped her hands together loudly and everyone stopped. "This is not how we behave! Have you forgotten you're in Class 6 now? You are meant to be setting an example for the rest of the school! I'll have that photo, thank you. Sita, you can collect it from me later. And if I hear anyone making donkey noises or talking about this photo there will be consequences. Am I understood?" she boomed.

"Yes, Miss," the class murmured.

Sita sat down in her chair, defeated. She had never felt so embarrassed. And now Sufi was even more upset with her. She'd only been trying to remind her of a happy time they'd had together. But instead, they felt even further apart. She noticed Kiri trying to nudge Sufi, but Sufi turned away. Sita could see that Sufi's eyes were all red. How was she ever going to make this better?

There was no time to think about it though, because Miss Malone wanted them to work on their projects.

"Right, Class 6. We have a lot of work to do! I've been told by the headteacher, Mr Bennett, that we are going to present our projects to the rest of the school next week!"

A groan rippled across the room. Sita didn't know anyone who liked talking in front of other people. Except Valentino, who shouted, "Yes!" and practically leaped out of his chair.

"Sit down," Sita muttered under her breath. "Chill out!"

Valentino looked at her, surprise on his face. "It's exciting though. Our presentation is going to be the best!"

"You don't know that. Plus, I'm terrible at presenting," Sita told him.

"We can work on that," V offered. "I have loads of tips. Rule number one is to imagine everyone in fancy dress! Rule number two: don't look down. Wait, I think that's for something else …"

Sita groaned to herself but said, "Really useful tips. Thanks."

Dina nudged her. "It'll be okay."

"I know … it's just a presentation," Sita replied.

"Not that. I meant it'll be okay with the whole photo thing.

Everyone will have forgotten about it by lunchtime," Dina said kindly.

"Oh, that. I don't care about everyone else. Sufi looked so angry with me. That's the second time this week I've annoyed her that much," Sita said sadly.

"What, like she never annoys you?" Dina asked.

"Not really," Sita said, but she wondered if that was actually true.

Miss Malone gave them the rest of the lesson to work on the project and it ended up being quite fun. Sita, Dina and V agreed on making a poster to present in the assembly. They each took responsibility for a section, and it was fun drawing out the different headings and putting in some of the information they'd already gathered. They were going to the library and community centre after school, and V's nan had arranged for them to speak to some of the people there about the area. Sita had said she'd bring snacks to keep them going. Dad had given her a large box of cereal bars and some grapes to share.

Kiri kept making donkey noises and Sita still felt upset about what had happened with the photo, but she found she was having fun with Dina and V. Kiri started to sound silly after a while anyway.

CHAPTER FIVE

At home time, Sita, Dina and V got ready to walk to the library and community centre. Sita had decided she wouldn't bother waiting for Sufi to tell her what she was doing because for the last two days Sufi had walked home with Kiri anyway. But as the three friends picked up their bags to leave the classroom, Sufi called out Sita's name.

"Hey, Sita, wait up!" she said.

Sita looked at Dina and V. "One second. You both start walking and I'll catch you up, okay?"

Dina raised an eyebrow. "Are you sure? We can wait for you."

"No, it's fine – I'll be right there, I promise. I know where the library is. Honestly, go on ahead. I'll be okay."

Dina and V looked at each other, seeming unconvinced, but they did as she asked.

As they walked off, Sufi came over. "Want to walk home together today?" she asked brightly, like nothing had happened over the last few days.

"I can't, I'm going with Dina and V to the library and community centre to work on our project. Plus, after what happened with the photo, I didn't think you'd want to talk to me at all. I am sorry about that, by the way."

Sufi shook her head. "Oh, I know. I can see you were trying to do a nice thing. Just maybe keep the rest of our childhood photos to yourself, okay?" She nudged Sita in the ribs playfully.

"Oh, okay, yeah, of course. Aren't you walking home with Kiri today?"

"She has football practice," Sufi said. "You'd better go – you said you had to go and work on your project. I guess I can just walk alone."

Sita felt bad then. "I can walk with you for a bit," she offered. "I'll just cut through the park to get to the library. Dina and V can start without me."

"Really, are you sure? That would be so nice," Sufi said, smiling. "I feel like we haven't hung out this week."

Sita wanted to reply, "Well, that's not my fault!" but she just smiled and nodded, which didn't feel good at all. She pushed the bad feeling away as they started walking.

Sufi chatted away about everything under the sun – the holiday to Spain her family had booked, the new bike she was getting for her birthday, the videos she'd seen online about how to French braid your own hair, and the online quiz that told you which princess you were most like. Sufi was obviously the one with the kind heart who could sing to animals. Sita wanted to laugh at that because Sufi was scared of most animals.

The whole time Sufi was talking, she didn't ask Sita one single question. But Sita decided she didn't mind, not really. It was just nice to be around Sufi. They sat on a wall and shared the cereal bars and grapes Sita had in her bag.

They were meant to be snacks for her, Dina and V, but she was sure the others would have packed some snacks for the library too.

As they sat there, Sita felt suddenly brave and asked, "What do you like about Kiri?"

She thought Sufi might get annoyed that she was bringing Kiri up, but she just smiled and said, "She's cool, you know? And she makes me feel cool. That's all."

Sita shook her head. "But you're different around her, like since when do you like tuna?"

Sufi sighed, "You don't understand, Sita. Sometimes it's not about what you like."

Sufi was right: Sita didn't understand at all.

Sufi chatted on and on for a while and it was only when Sita checked her watch that she realised how long they had been sitting on the wall for.

"Oh no, it's already been an hour. I was supposed to go straight to the library!" she cried.

Sufi shrugged. "I'm sure those two have been doing the work. They'll be fine."

"It's a group project, Sufi. I'm supposed to be there too. I have to go!" Sita said, jumping down off the wall. "I'll see you tomorrow. Maybe we can have lunch together?"

Sufi smiled. "Yeah sure, maybe."

Sita grabbed her bag and ran. She was out of breath by the time she reached the library. It was 4:25 p.m. – she was so late!

She ran in through the double doors and looked around. On the left was a big entrance to the library and on the other side was the community centre. She ran into the library and saw Dina and V straight away, sitting at a table with papers spread out in front of them. They didn't look impressed at all.

"I'm so sorry!" Sita said, plonking her bag on the floor and sitting down on an empty chair.

"What happened?" Dina asked quietly without looking up.

"Sufi and I ... we just got talking, that's all. I lost track of time," Sita said.

"You knew we were waiting, Sita," V said.

"I said I'm sorry and I'm here now. What can I do to help?" Sita asked. "I'll make it up to you, I promise. What can I do? Anything? Shall I do a silly dance?" she asked, wiggling on her chair. "I could do a handstand, although the last time I tried to do one, I gave myself a nosebleed and I don't think you want that."

She could see Dina was trying not to smile. "We've started a lot of the work, but I guess you can help with interviewing some of the people who use the community centre. Do you have the snacks? I'm starving!"

Sita gasped. "I ... we ... me and Sufi, I mean – we ate them. I'm so sorry. I thought you would bring some too, so it would be okay."

"Are you kidding me? You're an hour late *and* you shared our snacks with your so-called best friend who ditched you?" Dina was raising her voice now.

Valentino stood up. "It's okay Dina, I can ask my nan. She usually keeps some biscuits in the office."

"That's not the point, V," Dina said, still staring at Sita.

V tapped her shoulder. "I know, but she said sorry, and we need to finish our work, so let's forget it for now. I'll get the biscuits and you catch Sita up on what we've done already."

Sita shifted uncomfortably in her chair as Dina sat back down. "I really am sorry," she whispered. "I was just so happy that Sufi wanted to talk."

Dina ignored her and started talking about the project. "So, we've stuck in some photos of the library and community centre from when they were first built and then we've taken some on V's camera of how the buildings look now to compare. His nan is going to introduce us to two people who've been coming here since it opened so that we can hear how things have changed."

Sita swallowed hard. "Oh, umm, okay. I can write stuff down if that helps?"

Dina nodded and then said, "You know, Sita, you have two friends here who were waiting for you. I don't know what's so great about Sufi anyway."

Sita stared at the floor. "She's my best friend – I can't just ignore her."

Just then, V came back carrying a tray filled with snacks. "I guess my nan keeps more than a few biscuits in the office! She's coming over in a second and she'll take us to meet her friends Ali and Martha."

"Cool! I'm glad I didn't miss this bit," Sita said, and she meant it.

V's nan was not quite what Sita expected. She was wearing bright pink jeans and a flowery blouse. She had large hoop earrings and a big beehive bun hairstyle that wobbled on her head as she walked. She beamed at Sita and Dina. "Let me guess, you're V's new friends that I've been hearing so much about!"

Sita blushed. "Nice to meet you, Mrs ..."

V's nan scoffed, "Mrs nothing – call me Viv!"

Sita wasn't used to calling grownups by their first names. At home she had to call everyone Aunty or Uncle, even if they weren't related. It had never made sense to her.

Viv showed them all round the library and community centre.

"I can't believe I've never been in here," Dina said.

"Me neither," Sita admitted.

"Oh, it's just the nicest place. Valentino spends all his spare time here ... probably too much. I keep telling him to go outside and get some fresh air!" Viv laughed. "It's nice to see him with people of his own age!"

"Nan!" Valentino groaned.

"I'm just saying, friendships are important."

"Yes, Nan, I know. You tell me all the time," V sighed. "Friends are important."

"Ah, but what sort of friends?" Viv prodded him.

"The right sort of friends," V answered.

"And what kind of friend should you be?" Viv asked.

"The kind of friend I would want others to be to me," V replied. He looked at Sita and Dina who were grinning, finding the whole exchange quite funny. "Nan's big on friendship if you hadn't guessed. She's been drilling this stuff into me ever since I snatched a puzzle piece off another child."

"You didn't, did you?" Sita asked, amused.

"I was three and at nursery!" V protested.

"You're never too young to know how to be a good friend. Remember that girls, okay!" Viv said solemnly to Sita and Dina.

"We will," Dina replied, looking straight at Sita.

Later, they met Martha and Ali, Viv's friends of 35 years. That seemed like forever. Sita thought about Sufi and how they'd always said they would be best friends forever. She was glad things were okay with Dina and V now, but Sufi had actually wanted to spend time with her today after school. Maybe there was still a chance for Mission Friendship to succeed ...

CHAPTER SIX

That night at home, Dad asked how Sita's day had been. She told him about the photo and about how she'd upset Dina and V.

"I'm sorry it's been so hard, sweetheart," Dad said, hugging her. "I know how much Sufi means to you, but ..."

"But?" Sita said, looking up at Dad.

"Well, you know, I've been thinking about you and Sufi and I remembered that this isn't the first time she's done this," Dad said slowly.

"What do you mean? We've always been best friends – we never fall out."

"Mmm, that's not exactly true, Beta. Have you forgotten when she ignored you and didn't play with you for a whole week in Class 2? She said it was no big deal. But it *was* a big deal to you, and you were so upset."

"Oh," Sita said quietly.

"And what about the time she just stopped talking to you for two days, and when you asked her what was wrong she pretended it was all in your head?"

"I overreacted that time ..." Sita started to say, but deep down she knew she hadn't.

Sita thought about phoning Sufi to chat, but in the end, she decided not to. This past week, Sita had felt like she was losing her best friend in the whole world. And the worst thing was, she wasn't exactly sure how it had happened. Sufi just suddenly seemed to want to be one of the cool kids, like Kiri.

Wait – that was it. Sita needed to be cool too! Maybe then Sufi would want to be her friend again. It was a long shot as Sita had no idea how to be cool, but she was willing to try. One last attempt for the mission.

V's nan had said you should be the kind of friend you want others to be to you. Sufi wanted a cool friend, so Sita was going to be that friend. Mission Friendship was back on track! All she had to do was figure out what being cool actually meant!

Sita spent the whole evening trying to find information on how to be cool. None of her books were of any use – most of them only had the message to be yourself, and Sita had tried that already. She couldn't ask Dad – he was great for most things, but being cool was not one of them! Sita shuddered as she remembered Dad's terrible attempts at dancing at her last birthday party. Nope, asking Dad was not an option. Who else did she know that was cool?

She suddenly remembered Amy Lu, the girl influencer that Sufi liked. Amy Lu recorded videos on the latest fashion, hairstyles and music trends – proper cool stuff. If there was one person who could help Sita become cool, it had to be Amy Lu. Sita borrowed Dad's tablet and began looking up Amy Lu's tween tips vlog.

The first few videos weren't helpful – unless you wanted to learn how to curl your hair using random household items. Sita wasn't sure Dad would approve of her using his shaving cream like that! Then she found what she was looking for: Amy Lu's top tips for looking effortlessly cool. And tomorrow was non-uniform day at school. This was the perfect opportunity for Sita to show Sufi she could be just as cool, if not cooler, than Kiri.

When Sita explained this to V the next morning in the playground, he didn't look convinced. "I don't think that is what Nan meant, Sita. You should be yourself. Why would you change for someone else? And what is this outfit?"

"I'm doing it because Sufi has changed, so maybe I need to change too. We've always fitted together, and we don't right now, so if I change and become a bit cooler, we might fit again!" Sita said brightly.

Although as she said it, it didn't really sound exactly right. "And the outfit is almost exactly what Amy Lu said is this season's trendiest look!"

"You're wearing a bright green T-shirt, your hair is all wild and those boots look way too big!" V replied, looking Sita up and down sadly.

"Well, I didn't have a top in forest green, so this is the closest thing! And Amy Lu said natural curls are in, so I borrowed my aunty's hairdryer and it made my hair go all big. And I didn't have any hi-top trainers, so I wore my dad's boots. He's only like six sizes bigger than me. It's fine – I feel good!" Sita said, nodding her head vigorously, which made her hair bounce around.

She continued, "Amy Lu says the best way to be cool is to be your best self. When you look good, you feel good, and everyone else will see that confidence and want to be your friend! Okay, well I added that last bit, but it makes sense, don't you think?"

V shook his head. "I feel like this is going to go very wrong, Sita. Just saying."

"What's going wrong?" Dina asked as she walked over to them. "Oh, wow, Sita!"

Sita ignored Dina's shocked face and decided it was time to put part two of this step of Mission Friendship into action. Amy Lu said the next important thing to do if you wanted to be cool was to be friendly to everyone and offer them food. Sita decided that was a sure-fire way to be popular, and then everyone would want to be her friend. Including Sufi!

Sita pulled the plastic tub she had packed this morning out of her backpack.

"What's that?" V asked.

"Scrambled egg baps!" Sita replied happily. "Breakfast is the most important meal of the day, and this is going to help everyone love me!"

Sita skipped over to a group of Class 3 children standing by a bench. "Hi, I'm Sita. Would you like a breakfast bap?"

One of the boys screwed up his nose and said, "What's that smell?"

Sita looked down at the plastic tub. "They're egg sandwiches! Would you like one?"

One of the other children squealed, "Ew, eggy smell, I'm going to be sick!" and they all moved away.

Sita couldn't understand it – egg sandwiches were her favourite!

Sita looked around and saw Dina and V gawping at her. She wasn't going to give up though. She spotted Kiri and Sufi walking through the gates together. She needed to be cool. She needed Sufi to see her being cool.

This was it – her last chance. Sita shook her head like in the shampoo adverts and her big hair bounced about.

Sita walked casually past Sufi and Kiri towards India and Violet from Class 6C. Everything seemed to slow down. She could feel Sufi notice her. *Be cool, just be cool,* Sita told herself.

She opened the plastic tub, ready to offer a delicious egg sandwich to India, but she didn't notice her lace was undone. Suddenly, Sita tripped on her shoelace and lurched forward. The egg sandwiches flew out of the tub and up into the air, over the school gates and came down to land in a tree! Sita sprawled face first on the ground and noticed she was now sprinkled with bits of egg. Not cool. Not cool at all.

People were laughing at her. This was not what she'd meant to happen. Sita could feel her cheeks burning.

Dina and V were beside Sita within seconds to help her up. Sita looked around to see if Sufi had seen. Of course she had. Kiri was laughing and pointing.

Dina sighed. "Sita, I know you want Sufi to come back to you, but I feel like she doesn't even care that you might be hurt."

"You don't know what you're talking about," Sita said, clenching her jaw.

"I know that me and V are right here, wanting to be your friends, and you're treating us like Sufi treats you," Dina snapped.

Sita blinked hard. Was Dina right?

Kiri must have noticed what was going on, as she shouted out, "Aw, what's wrong, Dina? Are the losers having a fallout? Did your one friend finally realise what a loser you are?"

Sita looked at Dina who was staring hard at the ground, as if to stop herself crying.

Kiri carried on, "You know, Dina, don't worry. Sita won't stop being your friend, 'cos she's a total loser too!"

Sita glanced over at Sufi. She looked horrified but was just standing there. Was she really going to let Kiri carry on like this? The teachers were nowhere to be seen, probably still in the staff room. Some of the other kids in the playground were listening to Kiri's rant now, but everyone was too afraid to stand up to her. Dina looked so upset. V put his arm around her shoulder to comfort her.

Kiri laughed. "Aw, look, Valentino is looking after his girlfriend! I'm surprised—"

But Sita didn't let Kiri finish. Enough was enough. She remembered that Amy Lu's final piece of advice had been to stick to your principles – the things you believed in.

Sita stepped forward and yelled, "Just stop, Kiri. Stop being a bully! I thought I needed to be cool like you for Sufi to be my friend again, but you know what I've realised? You're not cool! Not even a little bit. You're just a big bully. Dina and V are my friends and I'm not going to let you talk to them like that any more." Sita let out a big breath. She couldn't believe she'd just said all of that.

Neither could Kiri, by the confused look on her face. She stood frozen for a second in shock and then murmured, "Whatever! It was just a joke anyway."

Sita turned to Dina and V. "Are you okay?" she asked.

Dina hugged her. "You were amazing!"

V smiled. "Nice to see the real Sita finally turn up."

"I'm sorry I've been so hung up on getting Sufi back. I was wrong. You were right, Valentino, I shouldn't change myself for anyone. Your nan said to be the friend you want others to be to you. She didn't mean change into what they want you to be. I had it *sooo* backwards."

"Finally, she gets it!" Dina laughed.

Just then, Sufi came over. "Hey, Sita, can I talk to you?" she asked.

Dina raised an eyebrow, but Sita said, "Sure, let's go over by the bench."

Sufi smiled. "You know, I thought that was pretty cool what you did just then, standing up to Kiri."

"I thought you *loved* Kiri these days?" Sita said.

Sufi looked uncomfortable. "I mean, she's okay, but it's not like how we are. She talks a lot about herself, to be honest."

Sita had to hide a smile. "Oh right, yeah, that would be super annoying."

"Do you think, maybe, we could hang out after school today? I've really missed that," Sufi said.

Sita glanced over at Dina and V. They were doing a terrible job of pretending they weren't watching her. "I have plans after school today," she said.

"Oh, okay," Sufi replied, clearly disappointed. "Maybe another time?"

Sita looked at Sufi. "Yes, maybe. But you really hurt my feelings this past week, Sufi. I'm not sure it can be like it was again."

Sufi sucked in a big breath. "Wow, you've changed, Sita."

Sita smiled. "I know. It feels kind of good. It feels more like I am being me. I'm going to go back over to Dina and V now, okay? I'll see you around." Sufi just stood there as Sita ran over to her friends.

And for once, Sita didn't feel bad. She knew she'd done the right thing.

She walked into class, sharing a group high-five with Dina and V. It felt like everything was going to be okay. No, better than okay. Everything was great.

Now answer the questions …

1 Who was Sita paired with for the class project?

2 Why did Sita think Kiri 'wasn't as over as Sita would have liked' on page 10?

3 What does 'curiously' mean on page 24?

4 What did you think would happen when Sita took the photo of her and Sufi wearing fancy dress into school?

5 What happened when Sita walked home with Sufi instead of going straight to the library with V and Dina?

6 Why did Dina look 'shocked' on page 54?

7 How did Sita's relationship with Valentino change from the start to the end of the story?

8 How did you feel about the way Sufi treated Sita during the story?